PULANE PHOKA

EPHEMERAL BEGINNINGS

How a Brief Encounter Can Redefine Your World

First edition

This book was professionally typeset on Reedsy.
Find out more at reedsy.com

Dedicated to...

To everyone who has ever felt lost in the shadows—May you find the courage to reclaim your light and the strength to write your own story.

This journey is for all of us.

"And the day came when the risk to remain tight in a bud was more painful than the risk it took to blossom."

— Anaïs Nin

Contents

Introduction

Life has a way of surprising us, often leading us down paths we never intended to travel. For me, it was a journey through heartbreak, self-doubt, and a seemingly endless search for validation. I was so consumed by the idea of being loved by someone else that I forgot to love myself first. My story is not unique—many of us have faced moments where we lost sight of who we are, clinging to people, habits, and ideas that do not serve us. But within those moments of loss, there is also the opportunity for growth and transformation.

This book is a collection of chapters from my life, each one a testament to the power of resilience, self-discovery, and the unyielding pursuit of self-worth. From the pain of unrequited love to the liberation of setting boundaries, I've learned that the most challenging experiences often lead to the most profound lessons. I've had to confront my fears, let go of unhealthy attachments, and rebuild my life from the ground up. Along the way, I discovered that true empowerment comes not from external validation, but from within—from the ability to reclaim your own story and write it on your own terms.

The chapters that follow are more than just a recounting of my experiences; they are a roadmap for anyone who has ever felt lost, stuck, or unsure of where to turn next. Through my journey,

I hope to show you that it is possible to rise from the ruins, to transform pain into purpose, and to emerge stronger and more resilient than ever before. You don't have to be defined by your past—you can choose to redefine yourself, to set new goals, and to pursue the life you deserve.

As you read these chapters, I encourage you to reflect on your own journey. What are the habits, relationships, or beliefs that are holding you back? What can you let go of to make room for growth? And most importantly, how can you reclaim your own story and begin writing the next chapter of your life with intention and purpose?

This book is for anyone who has ever struggled to find their way, who has ever doubted their worth, or who has ever wondered if they could truly start over. It's a reminder that you are stronger than you think, more resilient than you know, and more capable of change than you could ever imagine. So, let's begin this journey together—one chapter at a time.

* * *

I

Part One

In love and in doubt

1

Chapter 1

The unexpected encounter

What would you do if a brief encounter changed everything you thought you knew about love and yourself?

There I was, a third-year college student with white braids,quiet, reserved, the girl everyone thought they had figured out. My daily ritual involved a trip to the library, a place where I could lose myself in books. But that day, as I was deep in thought, a voice sliced through my solitude: "*Hey! How are you?*"

I looked up, and there he was—a face I had never seen before, someone completely new to me. Yet, there was something about his smile, something that drew me in. It was the kind of smile that could brighten even the dullest day. We exchanged numbers, and just like that, a new chapter in my life began.

Five days passed, and I found my thoughts increasingly occupied by him—let's call him Luna. There was something about Luna that made it impossible to get him out of my head. It's funny how the more you think about someone, the deeper the emotions grow, almost as if those thoughts have a life of their own.

He told me he wanted to get to know me better, suggested we go on a walk, maybe grab some chips. My heart raced at the thought. I was already imagining what I'd wear, how I'd style my hair. But just when I thought I had it all figured out, he threw in a twist.

"*Maybe you could visit me on Saturday, and we can do Netflix and chill*," he suggested. It was a classic line, the kind you hear and immediately question. Was this really about getting to know me, or was there something else at play? I knew the type—guys who wouldn't spend a dime but expected more than just a conversation in return.

But here's the thing—I couldn't see it. To me, all those warning signs were invisible. Red flags? They looked like lilac, and lilac was my favorite color. Still, I wasn't about to make it easy for him. I told him it would be difficult for me to come over, expecting him to back off. But instead, he surprised me.

He calmly suggested we take a walk on Sunday instead. I couldn't help but wonder—was this guy different, or was he just playing a more subtle game?

I realize how easily we can be blinded by excitement. It's a powerful emotion that can cloud judgment and make us ignore the signs that are right in front of us. But I've learned that it's essential to remain grounded, to question intentions, and to trust your instincts. Not everything that glitters is gold, and sometimes, the brightest smile can hide the darkest intentions.

As the days passed, I couldn't stop thinking about Luna. His easy smile and calm demeanor left a lingering impression on me, but I wondered if it was genuine or if I was simply reading into things too deeply. Sometimes, the thrill of meeting someone new can blind us to the subtle signs that tell a truer story. What if my curiosity about him was more about filling a gap in my own life than about who he really was?

Sunday, 14th May, arrived, and with it, a question that lingered in my mind: *Would Luna turn out to be everything I imagined, or was I stepping into something completely unexpected*?

* * *

2

Chapter 2

The First Impressions

Could it be 2 PM already? I found myself pleading with the clock, but time, as always, seemed to have its own agenda—moving at a snail's pace, mocking my anticipation. I was desperate to fast-forward through the day, to leap straight into the moment I'd been waiting for.

The morning light barely touched the horizon when I shot out of bed, my mind already buzzing. I did what any rational person does when nervous energy takes over: I turned to Google. "Questions to ask on a first date." Yes, I know, it sounds ridiculous, right? But when the stakes feel this high, you leave nothing to chance. Preparation is everything, and that day, I was on a mission to be perfectly prepared.

I carefully curated my look, every detail meticulously chosen to make an impression. My best outfit, my go-to handbag, my favorite lip gloss—nothing was left to chance. And the final touch? My signature perfume, the one that lingers just long enough to leave a memory. Nails? Flawless. I was ready. I had to be, because everyone knows, first impressions are everything.

Finally, the time came, and there he was, waiting for me, sitting with an air of calm confidence. The moment our eyes met, he stood and hugged me, and just like that, my nerves melted away. We began to walk, and as we did, I couldn't help but study him. He's a devoted Christian, deeply compassionate—a last-born with a shy demeanor that only added to his charm. And oh, that charm... it was disarming, to say the least. My mind was racing, yet all I could manage was a smile. Confused? You have no idea.

As the conversation flowed effortlessly, I realized that life often places the most unexpected people in our paths at the most unexpected times. It's easy to dismiss them, to convince ourselves that they don't fit the mold of what we think we want. But sometimes, the universe knows better than we do. Sometimes, it's in the moments of confusion and doubt that we learn the most about ourselves—what we truly need, not just what we think we desire.

People often say if you know what you want, you should go after it with everything you have. But what they don't tell you is how easily you can be led astray—how distractions sneak in, veering you off course before you even realize it. And then there are those opportunities, the ones that arrive silently, slipping through the back door when you least expect them.

Luna wasn't who I thought I wanted, not by a long shot. But there was no denying the electricity between us. We just... clicked. And in that moment, a thought I hadn't dared to entertain before took root: Could he really be the one?

As we walked and talked, I noticed little things about Luna—the way he tilted his head slightly when he was deep in thought, the way his laughter seemed genuine, almost unguarded. Yet, there were moments when I felt an invisible wall between us, a hesitation in his words that I couldn't quite place.

It made me think about how first impressions often feel like the opening act of a play. They're carefully crafted, polished, and presented to draw you in. But what about the hidden parts of ourselves—the ones we keep tucked away until we feel safe enough to share? Was Luna giving me his truth, or was this his best performance?

The thought lingered as I replayed our conversations in my mind later that night. Perhaps the most intriguing thing about meeting someone new isn't what they reveal but what they choose to hide.

I've come to understand that life's greatest lessons aren't always found in the grand gestures or the meticulously planned moments. Often, they're hidden in the small, seemingly insignificant experiences that catch us off guard. It's in those moments of spontaneity, when we let go of expectations, that we open ourselves up to the possibilities we never imagined. And maybe, just maybe, the things we never thought we needed turn out to be the very things that change our lives forever.

CHAPTER 2

* * *

3

Chapter 3

The One Who Knows You Best

You know that one person who holds your deepest secrets? The one who you can call at 2 AM when the tears just won't stop, and the chaos in your heart feels too overwhelming to bear? If you don't have that person in your life, well, maybe it's time to be that person. After all, we attract what we radiate, right?

For me, that person is Senate. The moment confusion clouded my brain, she was the first one I called. What did she do? She laughed! Can you believe it? Yep, she laughed and told me to calm down. "Relax," she said. And you know what? She was right. Nothing is as serious as we think—not in this world, anyway!

Her words stayed with me long after we ended the call. It struck me how often we seek advice from others not because we don't know what to do, but because we want confirmation of what we already feel. Senate had always been my anchor, the voice that brought me back to myself when I felt adrift.

Maybe that's why I kept turning to her during this whirlwind with Luna. She reminded me that while emotions are messy, they don't have to define your decisions. You can feel deeply and still choose wisely—a lesson I was just beginning to understand.

But let's get back to Luna. Sweet, sweet Luna. After ensuring I got home safe, he didn't just vanish into thin air. Oh no, he called, saying how much brighter I made his day. And let's be real—how can anyone not be charmed by that? Flattery at its finest! How do guys always know just what to say to make you feel like a queen?

Then came the silence. Luna and I didn't talk for a week. A whole week! I thought, "Well, that's the end of that." But honestly, I wasn't too bothered. It gave me time to explore other possibilities, to figure out what I really wanted. But then, out of nowhere, "*Hey, how are you?*"—there he was again, same place! He casually mentioned his birthday was the next day and hinted that my presence would be the best gift he could ask for!

Luna's charm was undeniable, but it also served as a reminder to stay grounded. The flattery and sweet words are nice, but they shouldn't cloud your judgment. In the end, the person who knows you best is yourself —the one who will always guide you true. Trust that voice, and let it lead you to the happiness you deserve.

Here's where the mind games began. "Is this his grand return?" I wondered. "Is this how he plans to sweep me off my feet again?" My thoughts raced. "Does he really want me there? Is this some VIP invite?" The internal debate was on! But then, I remembered what my younger self learned, "If you want real happiness, let your heart lead the way." And so, with a deep breath, I decided to follow my heart, wherever it might take me.

* * *

4

Chapter 4

The Kiss That Changed Everything

After I got my OS results script, there was only one thing on my mind: "Luna!" So, I zipped straight over to see him. "Happy birthday!, and *hakea u rekela letho*!" I beamed, cheekily admitting I hadn't bought him a gift. You see, I'm that girl who never quite mastered the art of money management—the one who's always chasing new experiences, indulging in a little too much fun. Money seems to slip through my fingers like sand, but hey, that's why I didn't get him anything. Also, in my defense, he did tell me about his birthday late!

We spent hours chatting about our families, and honestly, that's all I really remember. Did we talk about values or what we were both looking for in life? Nah, not a word. It's funny how you can spend all your time talking, and still not say anything that really matters. We were pros at that! But hey, sometimes it's not about the deep stuff; sometimes it's just about being.

Luna laughed—a lot. So much that it started to bother me. And not in a bad way, but in that "Why is this guy laughing at *Everything*?" kind of way. Let me explain: all the guys I know, whether friends, cousins, or neighbors, only laugh when something's genuinely funny. But Luna? He was laughing at almost everything I said! It's a blessing, really, because with people like that, you can just be your true, authentic self without any fear of judgment. People fighting inner battles often find joy in the little things—and they're usually the least judgmental.

Then came the time for me to leave. I told him I had to go, even though a part of me wanted to stay longer (he could tell too!). So, he suggested we take some pictures—*great* idea, right? We got closer and closer until our eyes met, our chins tilted ever so slightly, and then... BOOM! We kissed.

Now, before you ask, don't. Because I'm still trying to figure out what kind of kiss it was myself. It was one of those smoochy kisses that leave you feeling all kinds of things. And can I just say—*saliva? Eww*! But at the same time, I was like, "Okay, this feels kinda nice?" The whole thing still amazes me to this day.

But here's the kicker: that kiss wasn't just a kiss. It felt like the start of something—something I wasn't sure I was ready for, or even wanted. What did it mean? Was it just a moment, or was it the beginning of something more? As I walked away that day, my mind was racing, my heart was pounding, and one question kept echoing in my head:*What happens next*?

CHAPTER 4

* * *

5

Chapter 5

A Game of Silence and Obsession

I got home, charged my phone, and immediately dove into WhatsApp, eager to see if Luna had left me a message. He was online—my heart raced—but nothing, not a single word from him. What was this? A game of who breaks the silence first? I wasn't about to lose, but instead of feeling victorious, I ended up closing my eyes in a haze of confusion and exhaustion. It's funny how the silence from someone you care about can be louder than words.

The silence stretched on, heavy and suffocating. Each passing day felt like an eternity, as if time had slowed to taunt me. I hated how much power it had over me—how Luna's absence could consume my thoughts so completely.

It was in one of those quiet moments, staring at my phone, that

I had a realization: silence is never just silence. It's a space filled with all the things left unsaid, all the doubts and fears that creep in when the connection you crave is withheld.

But silence also has its own lessons. It forces you to confront the parts of yourself that you'd rather ignore—the insecurities, the need for validation. And maybe, just maybe, it teaches you to find strength in the stillness, to stop waiting for someone else to give you what you can give yourself.

Luna's inconsistency and my growing obsession with waiting for his messages revealed a harsh reality: when someone truly cares, they won't leave you guessing. Obsessing over someone's every move or word only leads to a downward spiral of confusion and insecurity. The lesson? Value your peace of mind more than the attention of someone who leaves you in doubt. In relationships, actions truly do speak louder than words—or silence.

A few years ago, I struggled to leave Facebook. The reason I wanted to leave so much was that there were so many opinions, and they were draining me emotionally. I also didn't like the amount of time I spent on the platform, endlessly scrolling through posts and updates. It felt like I was losing pieces of myself in the noise.

Then, things started to get better. I began taking week-long breaks from Facebook, and surprisingly, I felt fine during those moments of disconnection. It was during one of those better phases that I decided to log in again. And that's when I saw it—a friend request from Luna.

My heart skipped a beat. “Should I accept it? Should I ignore it?” I pondered for what felt like an eternity, but curiosity got the better of me, and I hit accept. Little did I know, that single click was the gateway to a whirlwind of pain, regret, and obsession. Sometimes, we chase what we think we need, only to find ourselves entangled in something we never wanted.

A few days later, on a Friday, Luna messaged me, asking if we could meet up at 4 PM. Of course, I said yes—I never could resist his invitations, even when they were last minute. He was late, but I didn’t mind. We met, exchanged pleasantries, and just like always, he said all the right things. Then, out of nowhere, he told me he liked me. To tell the truth, I liked him too, but I couldn’t admit it at that moment. I was confused—it felt as though things had moved way too quickly. So, I told him, “I can’t say anything right now; I think things are moving too fast,” and I left.

But when I got home, I couldn’t shake the thought. Why was I putting a time interval on feelings? I realized there was no need to wait to embrace something that felt real. So, I decided to tell Luna the truth—I liked him too.

As I sent the message to Luna, I didn’t realize it was the start of something far more complicated than I ever imagined.

6

Chapter 6

The Crossroads of Heart and Loyalty

As the end of lectures drew near, the exam countdown had officially begun. We were all getting busy, buried in books, and Luna? I would catch glimpses of him in the library. We didn't really call each other, just exchanged texts here and there. But, funny enough, I don't even remember if we wished each other good luck for the exams. After all,Maybe intentions aren't as important as results.

I found myself thinking about Luna often, and every so often, I'd check my WhatsApp, hoping for a reply, only to find those dreaded blue ticks. What was I saying wrong? Who knows! But then, one day, after leaving the exam hall, I did my usual WhatsApp check, and there he was—Luna had posted me on his status! That tiny gesture sparked joy in me like you wouldn't believe. Sure, my friends post me all the time, but somehow, this felt special. Sometimes, it's not *what* people do, but *who* does it that makes all the difference.

Exams finally ended, and with just one day left before I had to leave, I knew that if I didn't see Luna that day, it would be six long months before I'd get another chance. But fate, as usual, had its own plans. My friends wanted to hang out, and I had a hair appointment that took way longer than expected. By the time I was done, I had missed the time Luna and I had planned to meet. He called, but my phone was on silent mode—oops! I quickly called him back, apologized, and thankfully, we still managed to meet. Thanks, Luna!

We spent little time together because I was also going to see my friends. Yes, I couldn't let my friends down—I had promised to see them that day, and I am a big believer that promises must be kept! Besides, you can't go around disappointing your friends for someone you're not entirely sure about. Look at the stars," he said with a grin. We laughed. Though our time together was brief, it was fun. But then came the moment—he leaned in for a kiss. I hesitated and said no. It wasn't that I didn't want to, but it felt like he was trying to prove something, and I didn't want it to be that way. Instead, I hugged him, said goodbye and left.

The next morning, just as I was about to leave, Luna messaged me, wishing me a safe journey. And then... he told me he loved me. Wow. After saying no to his kisses? That was unexpected! But honestly? I wasn't surprised he wasn't heartbroken—after all, I wasn't his girlfriend yet. And to be fair, would it be that shocking if he wasn't completely devastated?

The brief time we spent together that evening was bittersweet.

I laughed at his jokes, held on to the fleeting warmth of his presence, but deep down, I knew it wasn't enough. A part of me was still clinging to the hope that he could be what I needed, even as another part whispered that it was time to let go.

I wanted Luna to be something he wasn't. I wanted him to choose me, to prioritize me in a way that made me feel secure. But loyalty isn't something you can demand—it's something freely given, or it means nothing at all.

Sometimes, the hardest decisions are the ones that force you to choose yourself over someone you love. But in that choice lies a quiet kind of strength—the kind that rebuilds you piece by piece.

Is it better to hold on to fleeting happiness or to walk away in search of something more lasting?

7

Chapter 7

A New Beginning

I told myself it was finally time—a chance to move on and leave Luna behind. His inconsistency weighed heavily on my mind, yet, ironically, the more I tried to distance myself, the more I found myself drawn to him. It was like an invisible thread pulling me back, no matter how hard I tried to break free. The more I missed him, the stronger the pull became.

As someone who thrives in the online world, Luna's lack of presence there created an emotional gap. It wasn't just about waiting for a message; it was the anticipation, the hope that maybe, just maybe, he'd reach out. But every day that passed without a word from him only deepened my obsession. I craved his attention more than I wanted to admit.

One day, he casually mentioned that I bored him. It stung, deeply. My mind spiraled into a whirlwind of self-doubt. Was

I too much? Too little? Was it me? Then, in a rare moment of clarity, I realized it wasn't about me at all—it was about him. His issues, his insecurities. I managed to muster a simple response, "Okay...cool," but inside, I made a promise to myself: I was done.

But promises to oneself can be hard to keep, especially when emotions are involved. A week or so later, Luna reappeared in my life, explaining that he needed to go offline to cope with personal struggles. He asked for space, and I gave it to him, hoping that he would come back better, stronger. When he did return, it felt like a victory. He was back, and so were the sweet messages, the words that made me feel special. We decided to make it official at the end of July—no more *situationship*, we were in a relationship now. It felt good, like everything was falling into place.

Situationships are messy. They're full of unspoken rules, emotional highs, and crushing lows. You're in it, but not really. It's like being caught in an emotional limbo where you're expected to feel but not show. And honestly, it's not healthy at all.

But life, as it often does, had other plans. My exam results were released, and I was eager to share my performance with Luna. Yet, when I tried to reach out, he was nowhere to be found. Offline, again. I left him a message, hoping he'd see it soon.

The next morning, as part of my routine, I checked his Facebook profile, only to stumble upon something unexpected—a post from someone wishing him a happy "Boyfriend Day." It was a surreal moment, one that left me laughing, not out of joy, but disbelief.

A lot of unsaid things started to make sense, at least to me, after seeing that post. Luna's inconsistency suddenly felt like more than just emotional turmoil—it was proof that there was something fishy all along. His coming and going, the sweet words followed by silence, and the carefully timed disappearances no longer seemed like a coincidence. It became clear that inconsistency isn't just confusing—it's often a mask, a way to hide the truth while keeping you emotionally tethered. And for the first time, I allowed myself to see it for what it was.

I closed the app, but the questions lingered, Was I walking away from chaos, or was I leaving behind a truth I couldn't handle? Either way, I knew I couldn't go back.

* * *

8

Chapter 8

New Norms of Modern Love

What if I told you that the abundance of choices in modern dating isn't liberating but paralyzing?In a world overflowing with options, many struggle to focus on just one person. Time feels fleeting, and opportunities seem endless. It's become the norm to juggle multiple connections simultaneously, each at different stages of dating. Some interactions are light and flirty, others more serious, while some remain undefined in "situationships." The focus on keeping options open often takes precedence over meaningful connection.

This phenomenon, rooted in psychology, is known as "loss aversion." It's the fear of letting go of even the faintest possibility of love, no matter how unfulfilling. Many people cling to individuals they aren't fully invested in, breadcrumbing them with just enough attention to keep them as an option. Call it fear, selfishness, or unconscious bias—it's a toxic pattern that reflects the complexities of modern relationships.

With everything swirling in my mind, I chose silence.I didn't ask Luna about that post,i didn't ask him about his cheating —not because I didn't want to, but because there was so much left unsaid between us. Words that should have been spoken long ago hung in the air, creating a fog of confusion. And confusion, as I learned, destroys trust. No one can believe in something that feels so uncertain. So, I told myself it was better to walk away and heal quietly. I tried to understand him, convincing myself I didn't need answers. Or maybe I was too afraid of what those answers would be. But staying silent turned out to be my biggest mistake. The doubts began to eat away at me, forcing me into an impossible choice: my values and self-respect, or the fragile remains of what we had. And in my vulnerability, I chose Luna.I had to choose between a hard way and an easy way. I chose the easy way, and like always, my life got hard.

Trusting him became difficult. I questioned everything he said or did. I'm not a competitive person, so instead of fighting to win him back, I slowly distanced myself.

Matters of the heart are tricky! After 2 months, despite knowing what I promised myself, I and Luna met. I was happy to see him. He bought me something small but meaningful. At that moment, I forgot what he did, or maybe I chose to. You can be convinced that you're over something, but your actions always reveal the truth. Mine did me worse—I said no to his kisses, no to almost everything he wanted us to do. I knew what I was doing; I just didn't know why.

To be clear, he didn't come back uninvited—I called him and set the date. Sometimes, people need to suffer the consequences of their actions, though at the time, I didn't realize what I was setting into motion. Unless people start clearly stating their values and are willing to change, relationships will always be considered hard, when in reality, they're not.

The Hard Truths of Easy Choices

The reality is, when we ignore red flags or silence our inner voice, we set ourselves up for heartache. The easy way isn't always the right way, and often, it leads to harder times ahead. Looking back, I see that by choosing to avoid confrontation, I was actually prolonging my pain. I learned that honesty—both with ourselves and others—is the foundation of any healthy relationship.

Setting boundaries isn't just about protecting yourself; it's about teaching others how to treat you. When we compromise on our values, we inadvertently tell others that it's okay to disrespect us. But the moment we stand firm on our principles, we begin to attract the respect and treatment we truly deserve.

We often forget that self-respect is the key to true happiness. No one can make us feel worthy unless we believe it ourselves. The path to self-love is paved with tough decisions and the courage to choose what's right over what's easy.

Love isn't a game, and relationships aren't about winning

or losing. They're about growth, mutual respect, and the willingness to be vulnerable without losing yourself in the process. And sometimes, the most loving thing you can do for yourself is to walk away.

In those quiet moments when Luna and I didn't talk, I found myself questioning everything—not just his intentions, but my own values. Why was I holding on to something so uncertain? And why did I feel like letting go would mean losing a part of myself?

The world of modern love is chaotic, a dance of fleeting connections and unspoken rules. It's easy to get caught up in the chase, to mistake attention for affection, and validation for love. But as I sat with my thoughts, I began to realize that love should never feel like a competition or a guessing game.

In the end, the person who truly knows you best should be you. When you know and love yourself, the right kind of love will naturally find its way to you—no breadcrumbs, no mind games, just real, unfiltered connection.

* * *

9

Chapter 9

The Realization

Picture a house being built on a shaky foundation—both the builders aware of its fragility but neither daring to speak the truth. Brick by brick, they continue, driven by hope, fear, and a silent desperation to see it finished. The foundation creaks under the weight, but they press on, pretending everything is fine. One builder skips days without explanation, and when he does return, he works in silence, indifferent.The other builder hesitates to question him, terrified that confrontation might drive him away, leaving the project abandoned. What will become of this house? Will it stand tall against the odds, or collapse under the weight of denial and misplaced effort?

This was the reality of my relationship with Luna. Instead of growing and evolving, we found ourselves locked in a cycle of stagnation. We barely spoke, reducing our connection to a rhythm of cold, three-day intervals—as though we'd signed some unspoken contract to stay just close enough to call it something. And yes, there were moments I wanted to scream, to tell him how his absence and distance tore at me. But fear always swallowed my voice.I feared the truth—that if I spoke, it would end, and I wasn't ready for that. Not yet.

Also,Luna seemed fine, comfortable with bread-crumbing me just enough to keep me hooked. Maybe, deep down, that was all he ever really wanted— to play games! Sometimes trying to understand the reason behind people's actions can be hard work!

Bit something strange happened,As the days passed, I noticed something unexpected. I didn't just love the attention, the routine of waiting for his messages—I loved him. The real him, or at least the version I thought was real. But the deeper I fell, the more painful it became. His care grew colder, and the distance between us widened.

Eventually, Luna and I stopped talking for two weeks. This time, he wasn't offline, and neither was I. I decided not to text him, hoping that this silence would help me move on. Yet, my heart grew heavier with each passing day. The anxiety returned, fueled by the last message he sent. I found myself stalking him online, checking his status obsessively. I knew I was attached, that this wasn't healthy.

But just as I started to convince myself that it was truly over, something unexpected happened—Luna posted a picture of me with a flower emoji as the caption. It was a small gesture, but it caught me off guard. Trying to make light of the situation, I sent him some laughing emojis, hoping to brush off the awkwardness. His response? "Are you still alive?" It felt so casual, so dismissive. Where was the respect, the acknowledgment of the time and emotions I had invested?

True to his promise, Luna tried calling me next. Unfortunately, my phone was on silent mode. I sent him a text explaining, but he didn't reply. I tried calling him the next day, mentally prepared for anything. When he finally picked up, I asked him one simple question: "Do you still want this? Us?" His response was typical—calm, assured, "Yes, why wouldn't I?"

What followed was a long conversation, filled with pauses and truths that had been buried for too long. In the end, Luna confessed that he no longer felt the same. He loved me, but not in the way that mattered. With that, I thanked him and said goodbye.

Luna was a master of words, always twisting them just enough to leave me wondering. He suggested starting over, wiping the slate clean. But it was obvious—we were on different paths, holding onto different values. In that moment, I made a choice. I blocked him, not out of spite, but out of self-respect. That night was heavy with emotions, but I knew deep down that this was a win. He may have chosen someone else, but I chose me, and that's what truly mattered.

As Luna's messages grew colder, I found myself spiraling into a cycle of self-doubt. What had changed? What was I doing wrong? It was a cruel kind of irony—that the more I sought his approval, the less I seemed to get it.

But in the silence that followed, something shifted. I realized that his behavior wasn't about me—it was about him. His inconsistency, his distance—they were reflections of his own struggles, not my worth. And while I couldn't control his actions, I could choose how I responded to them.

That realization was both painful and freeing. It taught me that love isn't about chasing someone's affection or proving your value. True love—whether from another or for yourself—comes without conditions, without games, without doubt.

Still, as I lay awake that night, I couldn't shake the feeling that Luna's words held more secrets than he let on. I had made my choice, but a question lingered: What if this ending wasn't the end? What if there was still more to uncover about the man I thought I knew?

* * *

10

Chapter 10

From Stalker to Goal-Setter

Now, what was left? This should have been the perfect moment to focus on what truly mattered—to rebuild, to rediscover myself. But life doesn't work like that. Reality is messy, and humans are emotional, not logical. We act on impulses, driven more by our hearts than our minds. And so, my thoughts, my energy, my very existence, were consumed by Luna. Every move he made, every glance, every word—it all became the axis my life spun around, as if the rest of the world had faded into nothingness.

I went so far as to create a fake account, spending my days stalking him and his other girlfriend. It became my daily routine, a job that drained my energy but never paid. I knew what I was doing was wrong, unhealthy, and self-destructive, but it felt like a way to stay connected to something I couldn't let go of.

Bad habits are easy to fall into but notoriously hard to break. If you're caught in this trap, I urge you to stop before it consumes you. The more you invest in these toxic behaviors, the deeper the damage goes.The best remedy is to replace those habits with something healthier.It's not enough to just stop—you need to choose something better, something that enhances your life rather than consumes it.

Realizing that my obsession was spiraling out of control, I knew I had to change. But simply stopping wasn't an option—I had to replace my bad habits with healthier ones. I started spending more time with friends and family, even though I often felt the urge to check up on Luna. I discovered that taking walks helped me observe my thoughts without acting on them.

I needed to shift my focus away from Luna and onto something positive. So, I set ambitious goals for myself. I promised to finish eight business books in a month while keeping up with schoolwork. I committed to hitting the gym at 5 a.m. on weekdays and made Sundays my "me time"—a day dedicated to fun and relaxation.

Achieving these goals wasn't easy, but it was incredibly rewarding. I started feeling more confident and learned to control my actions instead of being driven by unhealthy impulses. The gym became a sanctuary where I met great people who, like me, were there to improve their mental health, not just their bodies.

One day, while caring for my first plant, I asked myself, "Why not delete Facebook?" I realized it was just another avenue for my unhealthy habits, so I deleted it. And it was the best decision ever—at least for now. Taking control over that part of my life was a turning point.

As I began to reclaim my life, I even forgot Luna's phone number. When we finally crossed paths six months later, all he said was "hi," and that was it. It was like a weight had been lifted off my shoulders. I used to stress about how I would react when I saw him again.The anxiety I had built up around that moment vanished, and I realized how much time we waste worrying about things that will never happen.

If you find yourself drowning in obsessive behavior, it's essential to recognize and address it promptly. Indulging in unhealthy habits can trap you in a cycle that's hard to escape. Prioritize your mental well-being by replacing those habits with positive, fulfilling activities. Seek support if needed, and make conscious choices to build a healthier, more balanced life. Your mental health is invaluable, and it starts with taking proactive steps towards a better you.

I deleted Facebook and started focusing on my goals, it felt like I was finally taking back control of my life. I replaced the endless scrolling and obsessive checking with something far more fulfilling: progress.

Every book I read, every early morning at the gym, every quiet moment spent nurturing my plants—it all brought me closer to the version of myself I wanted to be. And as I poured my energy into these pursuits, the grip that Luna once had on my heart began to loosen.

Just as I began to feel whole again, I couldn't shake the thought—was this the calm before another storm?

* * *

11

Chapter 11

The Art Of Closure

I used to see Luna almost every day at the library. Our conversations were always brief, just polite nods and hollow greetings. On the surface, it seemed like we'd both moved on. But inside, I was a storm of questions and frustration. Why did he think it was okay to declare he was "over it" only after he'd already hurt me? The mystery of his actions was driving me mad.

Then, it happened. Lucky day! Luna came up to me out of the blue and asked how I was doing. He even asked why I blocked him. That was the golden ticket I'd been waiting for—the chance for closure. We decided to meet in a quiet spot on campus, no time wasted.

When we finally sat down, I dove right in. The first question on my mind: "Why aren't we together anymore?" Simple, right? But the way he answered would tell me everything I needed to know. Or so I thought

Luna looked me straight in the eyes, and what did he do? He lied. Immediately, disappointment washed over me. Luna didn't just lie; he blatantly disrespected me. He wasn't the person I thought he was—he wasn't even close. I realized in that moment that Luna didn't respect anyone, not even himself.

But hey, sometimes the truth doesn't hurt—it liberates. The second he admitted to lying, I felt this strange sense of relief. I laughed it off, thanked him for coming, and said goodbye. I was done. I got the closure I didn't even know I needed. Luna's lies didn't break me; they freed me.

The most amazing part? I woke up the next day feeling lighter, happier, and surprisingly... over it. It felt like I had been set free from the chains of confusion. And just when I thought it was all behind me, Luna showed up again—this time asking for some random, trivial help. It was obvious he was grasping at straws, trying to hold onto something that was long gone. I smiled, helped him out, and that was it. That was the last time I saw Luna.

The chapter wrapped itself up not with a dramatic flourish, but with a serene, satisfying realization: I was free. Free from the deception, the confusion, and the emotional turmoil. And you know what? It felt absolutely exhilarating.

When Luna finally admitted to lying, I felt an unexpected sense of relief. It was as if the weight of all my unanswered questions had been lifted, leaving behind a clarity I hadn't known I needed.

Closure doesn't always come in the form of a heartfelt apology or a perfect explanation. Sometimes, it's simply the moment you realize that you deserve better—that your worth isn't tied to someone else's actions.

As I walked away from Luna that day, I felt lighter, freer, and more at peace than I had in months. It wasn't just the end of a chapter—it was the beginning of a new one.

* * *

12

Chapter 12

Lessons of Love and Letting Go

There comes a time when the life you've built, brick by brick, with so much hope and love, crumbles before your very eyes. It's in that moment of collapse, when everything familiar disintegrates, that you're faced with a choice: Do you sift through the debris, trying to salvage what's lost? Or do you step back, take a breath, and begin to rebuild something new—something stronger, something entirely your own?

My relationship with Luna was a paradox—a beautiful dream wrapped in a harsh reality. He was my first love, the one who filled my days with laughter and my nights with endless conversations. But beneath the surface of our connection lay a deeper truth: I was losing myself in the process. I had allowed my identity to be overshadowed by my attachment to him, my sense of worth tied to his approval.

When it finally ended, the pain was undeniable. It felt like the world as I knew it had been torn apart, and I was left standing in the ruins of what once was. But a midst the heartbreak, I found something unexpected: clarity. I realized that I had spent so much time and energy trying to fit into Luna's world, trying to be what I thought he wanted, that I had neglected my own needs, my own growth. This clarity became the first of many lessons—one that taught me the importance of self-awareness and the dangers of losing oneself in the pursuit of love.

Letting go of Luna wasn't just about walking away from a relationship; it was about walking toward myself. It was about shedding the layers of insecurity and doubt that had been weighing me down for so long. It was about reclaiming the parts of me that I had lost in the pursuit of love. Through this, I learned the crucial lesson of self-acceptance, understanding that my worth isn't determined by someone a midst perception, but by how I perceive myself.

In the aftermath, I discovered a version of myself that I had long forgotten—a woman who was strong, capable, and worthy of all the good things life had to offer. I found joy in the simplest of things: nurturing my love for plants, diving into books that fueled my soul, and challenging my body in ways that made me feel powerful. Each day was a step forward, a step toward becoming the person I was always meant to be. This journey taught me that healing often comes from reconnecting with the things that bring you genuine happiness, those small passions that anchor you to your true self.

As I navigated this journey of self-redefinition, I set new standards for my life. I learned that setting boundaries is not an act of selfishness, but an act of self-respect. Blocking Luna wasn't just about removing him from my life; it was about removing anything that no longer served my growth, anything that kept me from fully embracing who I am. This was perhaps the most liberating lesson of all: that you must protect your peace, even if it means letting go of people or situations that no longer align with your values.

I no longer see the end of our relationship as a failure. Instead, I see it as the catalyst for the most significant transformation of my life. Through the pain, I found purpose. Through the heartbreak, I found healing. And through the loss, I found myself. Luna was not the enemy; he was the mirror reflecting back to me the areas where I needed to grow, the wounds that needed to be healed. He was the teacher who, unknowingly, guided me toward the greatest lesson of all: that true love starts from within.

When you're faced with the ruins of what once was, don't despair. See it as an opportunity to rebuild, to redefine who you are and what you stand for. Embrace the power of letting go—not as an act of giving up, but as an act of moving forward, of claiming the life that you deserve.

Rise from the ruins, stronger than before. Let the pain fuel your transformation, let the loss inspire your growth. And remember, the greatest love story you'll ever live is the one you write with yourself.

The hardest thing about letting go is accepting that some people are only meant to be part of your story for a season. Luna taught me so much—not just about love, but about myself.

Letting go was never easy, but it was necessary. I didn't just release Luna, I released the fears, the insecurities, and the self-doubt I had carried for so long. It was the most difficult decision I've ever made, but it gave me space to heal. What I didn't know was that this was just the beginning. This was the moment I started to truly reclaim myself.

Through the pain of our ending, I found strength I didn't know I had. I learned to set boundaries, to prioritize my happiness, and to trust that the right kind of love will find me when the time is right

And so, as I close this chapter of my life, I realize that every heartbreak, every setback, and every tear shed has led me here—to this moment of clarity and peace. The journey was not easy, but it was necessary. As I step into the next phase of my life, I do so with a heart full of gratitude, knowing that the lessons I've learned have shaped me into the person I am today.

* * *

II

The Science and Soul of Love

Love is rarely simple. It's a mix of unforgettable firsts, silent obsessions, and messy heartbreaks shaped by digital connections and blurred boundaries. In this part, we uncover how love consumes us, how social media traps us, and how we rebuild, revealing what love teaches us about ourselves.

13

Chapter 13

The Psychology of First Love

First love is often regarded as a defining milestone in human experience. It is intoxicating, consuming, and leaves an indelible mark on our psyche. According to Dr. Helen Fisher, an anthropologist renowned for her research on love, the brain reacts to first love similarly to how it responds to addictive substances. The reward system floods with dopamine, creating feelings of euphoria and attachment.

This explains why the memories of first love can linger vividly, even years after the relationship has ended. Neurological studies suggest that the adolescent brain, where first loves often occur, is particularly susceptible to these intense emotions due to heightened sensitivity in the brain's limbic system. This phase is crucial for emotional learning, and the experiences of love,both its joys and heartbreaks,shape our relational blueprints.

Psychologists like Dr. Susan Krauss Whitbourne assert that "the way we navigate first love often determines how we approach future relationships." Despite its romantic allure, first love is rarely sustainable. Sociologist Eva Illouz highlights that first love often fails because it exists more in fantasy than reality. Young lovers project their ideal selves and aspirations onto their partners, creating unrealistic expectations.

The disillusionment that follows is not a failure but a crucial step in understanding the complexities of adult relationships. The cultural idealization of first love also plays a role in its significance. Songs, films, and literature,ranging from Shakespeare's Romeo and Juliet to Taylor Swift's lyrics,reinforce its mystique. This societal narrative embeds first love as not just a personal experience but a universal rite of passage.

In reflecting on first love, it's essential to acknowledge its duality: both a source of immense joy and profound pain. As the poet Rumi once said, "The wound is the place where the light enters you." First love teaches us not just about others but about our capacity to grow, endure, and love again.

14

Chapter 14

In the Shadows of the Digital Age
(Stalking and Social Media)

The digital age has made connection easier but also magnified the shadows of relationships. Social media, while often a tool for connection, has become a double-edged sword in matters of the heart. For those experiencing heartbreak or navigating unrequited feelings, it can be both a lifeline and a trap.

Digital stalking, a behavior now normalized in modern relationships, is a frequent response to uncertainty or loss. Unlike traditional stalking, digital stalking operates subtly,checking someone's Instagram stories, analyzing who liked their posts, or revisiting old photos.

A 2020 study in *Computers in Human Behavior* revealed that 80% of people admitted to checking an ex-partner's social media after a breakup. This behavior is fueled by the brain's craving for information to fill emotional gaps.

Psychologically, this habit ties back to our need for closure. In the absence of direct communication, social media becomes a surrogate, offering fragments of someone's life that are easy to misinterpret. The curated nature of these platforms,where people post highlights rather than realities,can amplify feelings of inadequacy or longing.

As psychologist Dr. Tara Fields explains, "Social media creates a false sense of proximity, making it harder to let go of someone who is no longer truly present in your life."

The cultural acceptance of these behaviors stems, in part, from media portrayals. Movies and TV shows often romanticize obsessive behaviors as proof of love or devotion, further blurring the line between interest and intrusion. However, the emotional toll of digital stalking is real. A study published in *Journal of Social and Personal Relationships* found that excessive monitoring on social media is linked to increased anxiety, depression, and lowered self-esteem.

The solution lies in mindfulness. Understanding why we engage in these behaviors can help break the cycle. Are we seeking closure, reassurance, or control? Awareness of these motivations can lead to healthier coping mechanisms, such as journaling, therapy, or creating physical and emotional distance from triggers like social media.

As the poet Warsan Shire wrote, "You can't make homes out of human beings." Similarly, we cannot find peace by living in someone else's curated digital world. Letting go, though difficult, allows us to reclaim our emotional space and focus on personal growth.

15

Chapter 15

Healthy Values for Healthy Love

What distinguishes a healthy relationship from a toxic one? The answer lies in shared values, effective communication, and mutual respect. Dr. John Gottman, a leading relationship expert, identifies trust and commitment as the cornerstones of lasting love. Without these, relationships are unlikely to endure life's inevitable challenges.

Healthy relationships prioritize emotional safety. Partners should feel seen, heard, and valued. Brené Brown underscores the importance of vulnerability in fostering deep connections, stating, "Vulnerability is the birthplace of love, belonging, joy, courage, and empathy."

Self-love is also essential. You cannot pour from an empty cup. When individuals neglect their own needs, they risk resentment and burnout in relationships. As Oprah Winfrey wisely observes, "You are responsible for the energy you bring into a relationship." Finally, healthy love requires boundaries.

Boundaries are not walls; they are guidelines that define how we wish to be treated. Setting boundaries is an act of self-respect and teaches others to honor our needs. A healthy relationship is not without its challenges, but it thrives on collaboration, growth, and the willingness to navigate difficulties together. It is not about finding someone perfect but about building something enduring with mutual effort and care.

16

Chapter 16

The Role of Attachment Styles in Relationships

The way we love is often shaped long before we even understand what love is. Attachment theory, developed by psychologist John Bowlby, explains how early interactions with caregivers influence our emotional patterns and behaviors in relationships. Understanding attachment styles: secure, anxious, avoidant, and disorganized, offers a roadmap to healing and creating healthier connections.

Those with a *secure attachment* style tend to form healthy relationships. They trust their partners, communicate openly, and are comfortable with intimacy. This foundation often comes from consistent, loving care during childhood.

On the other hand, *anxious attachment* leads to fear of abandonment and excessive need for reassurance. Those with an *avoidant attachment* style may struggle to open up, avoiding emotional vulnerability. Finally, *disorganized attachment*, often rooted in trauma, results in a conflicting push-pull dynamic in relationships.

Dr. Amir Levine, in *Attached*: The New Science of Adult Attachment and How It Can Help You Find and Keep Love, explains that recognizing attachment style is the first step toward healthier relationships. For example, an anxiously attached person may overthink a partner's delayed text, interpreting it as rejection, while an avoidantly attached person may withdraw to protect themselves from perceived vulnerability.

By recognizing these patterns, we can break free from the cycle of unhealthy dynamics. Therapy, self-reflection, and mindful communication allow individuals to shift toward secure attachment, even if their early experiences were inconsistent or painful. As psychologist Mary Ainsworth noted, "Attachment is not destiny." Understanding your attachment style is not just about improving relationships with others—it's also about healing the relationship with yourself.

17

Chapter 17

The Power of Healing Through Creativity

Creativity is often the unsung hero of healing. Whether through writing, painting, music, or other forms of expression, creativity allows us to process emotions that words alone cannot capture. As writer Julia Cameron notes in *The Artist's Way*, "Creativity is a spiritual practice. It's not about making art; it's about making life."

After heartbreak, creative outlets become a safe space to explore pain without judgment. Writing, for instance, helps untangle the complexities of emotion. Studies in the *Journal of Psychosomatic Medicine* reveal that expressive writing can reduce anxiety and improve overall well-being by transforming trauma into a coherent narrative.

Art, too, offers a release. Abstract forms and colors allow emotions to flow freely, bypassing the need for logic or explanation. Music, whether creating it or simply listening, taps into the brain's reward system, flooding it with dopamine and lifting moods.

My journey of blogging and writing this book is a testament to the power of creativity. It turned my pain into purpose. Creativity teaches us that while we may not control what happens to us, we can always choose how to respond.

In the words of Elizabeth Gilbert, "You do not need anybody's permission to live a creative life." Healing through creativity is not about being perfect,it's about being present, allowing yourself to feel, and using those feelings to build something beautiful.

III

Part Three

In retrospect

18

Chapter 18

The Gift of time

As I reflect on everything, I can't help but wonder, What if I had walked away sooner? What if I had trusted my instincts earlier and not stayed as long as I did? Would I have learned the same lessons, or would the hurt have been avoided? Those are questions I'll never have the answers to, and in the end, I've come to realize that maybe it doesn't matter. What matters is what I gained from it all—the clarity, the growth, and the strength to walk away when it was time. But still, I wonder... What if?

The truth is, if I had left early, I wouldn't know the things I know now. That relationship, as painful and complicated as it was, taught me more about myself than I ever expected. It wasn't just about learning who Luna was; it was about uncovering who I am.

I became self-aware in ways I didn't even realize I needed to be. That relationship showed me the parts of myself I had ignored for so long—the insecurities I didn't want to admit existed, the pain I tried to bury, and even the simple things that genuinely bring me happiness. I learned what triggers me, what pushes me to the edge, and, more importantly, what pulls me back to peace.

It also taught me what I want in a partner—what I really want. Not the surface-level things, but the core values, the traits that make love not just passionate but sustainable. I now know what I won't settle for, what boundaries I need, and how to recognize when something isn't right for me.

If I had left early, I wouldn't have this book. This story wouldn't exist, because the lessons I've poured into these pages wouldn't have been learned. As much as it hurt, that relationship was the catalyst for growth I didn't even know I needed.

So, while I sometimes wonder how different things could have been, I'm at peace with the way it all unfolded. I stayed longer than I should have, but in doing so, I gained something invaluable: clarity, strength, and a story worth telling.

* * *

19

Chapter 19

Why Did I Stay Despite the Signs?

Why did I stay? That's the question that keeps hitting me when I look back. I'm not even sure I can answer it fully, but I'll try.

I loved him. And when you love someone, you do stupid things. I convinced myself that if I just stuck it out, if I just waited a little longer, things would change. But deep down, I knew the truth: we were heading in different directions. I could feel it, but I ignored it, because I didn't want to admit it to myself. The signs were right there, like a blinking red light. But I ignored it, convinced that love would somehow make everything work.

And then there was my ego. It wasn't about being right—it was about not admitting I was wrong. I couldn't apologize. I couldn't own up to my mistakes. Instead, I did what anyone with a bruised ego does: I blamed him for everything. The misunderstandings, the things that weren't working. It was all his fault.

Instead of sitting down with myself and taking a good look at where I messed up, I let my ego take the wheel. I wasn't ready to face the fact that maybe I was the problem. So, I kept blaming him, telling myself that if he just acted differently, things would be fine. I didn't realize it then, but that was a massive red flag. My ego kept me trapped in a cycle of pride and denial, and it stopped me from seeing the truth.

Obsession, though—that was the real killer. At first, it was just love, but somewhere along the way, it turned into something unhealthy. I would delete his number, tell myself it was over, but obsession doesn't work like that. It sneaks up on you, and before you know it, you're saving the number again, checking his socials, wondering if this time things will be different. You guessed it right, they never were. But obsession didn't care. It had me in a choke hold, making me think I could somehow fix it, even when I knew deep down it was already broken.

And honestly, like i said, I knew we didn't have a future together. We wanted different things, and I wasn't blind to it. Luna wasn't the man I dreamed about. He wasn't the guy I pictured by my side, standing strong and supporting me. He didn't know how to say no to me, and that right there was a problem. I didn't want someone who would always give in. I needed someone who stood firm, who wasn't afraid to challenge me, to make me think. But he didn't. He was too easily swayed by whatever I wanted, and that was the last thing I needed.

CHAPTER 19

* * *

20

Chapter 20

Notes from the Journey

As I leave these words behind and embrace what's next, I'm filled with gratitude—not just for the lessons, but for the journey itself. Because in the end, it wasn't about finding someone else. It was about finding myself

As I write this section, I find myself smiling—genuinely, fully. I'm at peace now, something I never thought I'd say about this story. What started as scribbles in my diary, a way to process my thoughts and emotions, has turned into something much bigger than I ever imagined.

At first, it was just for me—a way to make sense of the journey, the heartbreak, and everything in between. But then I lost my diary, and I realized I needed a way to capture these moments in a place that would last forever. That's when I created my personal blog, The *Enlightened Bookworm.* It became my safe space, a home for my reflections and lessons, a place to share not just my story but my growth.

And then something changed. People began to read my posts, and their responses overwhelmed me. They told me my words resonated with them, that my story helped them heal or see things differently. What started as a personal outlet became a bridge—connecting my pain and lessons to others who needed them.

That's when I realized this story needed to reach even more people. A book felt like the only way to make that happen. So, I started gathering the chapters, compiling the pieces of my journey, and shaping them into what you're holding in your hands now.

But here's the truth: I've never read this book from cover to cover. Every chapter, every page, was written from a place of heartbreak and pain. Revisiting those moments feels like opening an old wound, and there's still a part of me that's scared—scared of what those emotions might bring back.

Yet, through this journey, I've learned so much about love, loss, and life:

1. Love yourself first. No one will ever fill the gaps you haven't filled yourself. I spent so much time seeking validation from others when the truth was, I needed to find it within me. Love that starts with self-love is the kind that lasts.

2. Letting go isn't giving up.For the longest time, I thought walking away meant I'd failed. But I now know it means you're strong enough to leave what's not meant for you. Letting go creates space for healing and growth.

3. Obsession isn't love.Obsession consumes you—it twists reality and keeps you chained to something that isn't good for you. True love doesn't demand that you lose yourself.

4. Surround yourself with people who lift you.The friends who stood by me, who told me the hard truths when I needed to hear them, they're the ones who helped me heal. The people you choose to keep around you shape your journey in ways you can't imagine.

5. Trust your intuition. Deep down, I always knew when something wasn't right, but I ignored it. Your intuition is your inner compass—don't let it be drowned out by fear or doubt.

As I write these words, I feel an overwhelming sense of pride—not because this book is perfect, but because it's real. What was once just a thought, a fleeting idea, has become something tangible and meaningful. This book isn't just my story; it's proof that even in pain, there is purpose.

To everyone who has read this far, thank you. Thank you for letting me share my journey with you, for allowing my words into your life. My hope is that this book, born from my broken heart, can bring healing, strength, and inspiration to yours.

This isn't the end. It's just another beginning—for me, for you, and for anyone who needs a reminder that even in our darkest moments, we can find light.

The final word is spoken.

* * *

About the Author

Pulane Phoka, the voice behind "The Enlightened Bookworm," is a passionate writer who delves into themes of personal growth, resilience, and self-discovery. She aims to inspire others to find strength and wisdom in their own journeys.

You can connect with me on:

- http://www.bornitblogger.wordpress.com
- https://www.linkedin.com/in/pulane-phoka

www.ingramcontent.com/pod-product-compliance
Lightning Source LLC
LaVergne TN
LVHW040952150826
845672LV00002B/650

* 9 7 9 8 2 3 0 4 3 9 2 3 3 *